Lerner SPORTS

SPORTS
VIP s

MEET

AARON
RODGERS

SAM LASKARIS

Lerner Publications ◆ Minneapolis

SPORTS THRILLS *MEET* RESEARCH SKILLS

Lerner SPORTS

Free Database Trial: **lernersports.com**

Thanks to everybody who has provided guidance and support throughout a lengthy writing career.

Copyright © 2025 by Lerner Publishing Group, Inc.

Lerner Publications Company
An imprint of Lerner Publishing Group, Inc.
241 First Avenue North
Minneapolis, MN 55401 USA

For reading levels and more information, look up this title at www.lernerbooks.com.

Main body text set in Aptifer Slab LT Pro. Typeface provided by Linotype AG.

Editor: Nicole Berglund

Library of Congress Cataloging-in-Publication Data

Names: Laskaris, Sam, author.
Title: Meet Aaron Rodgers : New York Jets superstar / Sam Laskaris.
Description: Minneapolis : Lerner Publications, 2025. | Series: Lerner sports. Sports VIPs | Includes bibliographical references and index. | Audience: Ages 7–11 | Audience: Grades 2–3 | Summary: "Champion quarterback Aaron Rodgers played for the Green Bay Packers for 18 seasons before joining the New York Jets in 2023. Learn all about the career of this Super Bowl winner"— Provided by publisher.
Identifiers: LCCN 2023057933 (print) | LCCN 2023057934 (ebook) | ISBN 9798765626016 (library binding) | ISBN 9798765629758 (paperback) | ISBN 9798765637685 (epub)
Subjects: LCSH: Rodgers, Aaron, 1983-—Juvenile literature. | Quarterbacks (Football)—United States—Biography—Juvenile literature. | Football players—United States—Biography—Juvenile literature.
Classification: LCC GV939.R6235 L37 2025 (print) | LCC GV939.R6235 (ebook) | DDC 796.332092 [B]—dc23/eng/20231221

LC record available at https://lccn.loc.gov/2023057933
LC ebook record available at https://lccn.loc.gov/2023057934

Manufactured in the United States of America
1-1010134-51935-3/6/2024

TABLE OF CONTENTS

>>>>>>>>>>>>>>>>>>>>>

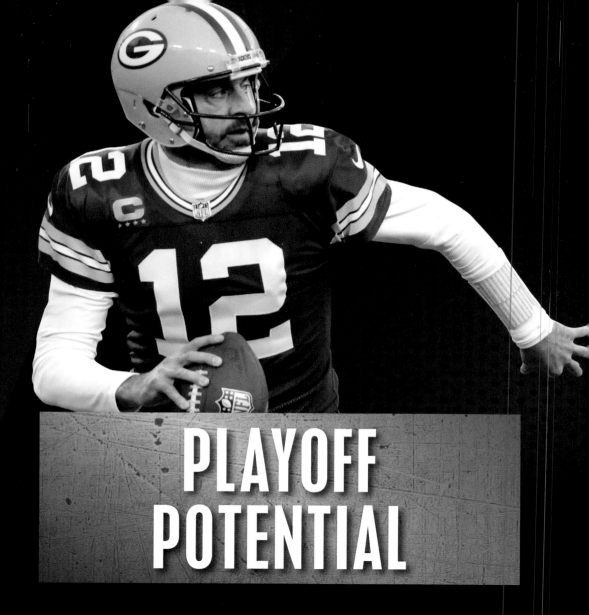

PLAYOFF POTENTIAL

January 1, 2023, was a big day for the Green Bay Packers. They were set to face one of their biggest rivals, the Minnesota Vikings. It was the second to last regular season game of the year. Green Bay needed a win to keep its playoff hopes alive for the season.

Football is a team game. But the Packers were really counting on one man to lead them to victory. That was their star quarterback, Aaron Rodgers.

FAST FACTS

DATE OF BIRTH: December 2, 1983
POSITION: quarterback
LEAGUE: National Football League (NFL)

PROFESSIONAL HIGHLIGHTS: won four NFL MVP awards; won the Super Bowl in 2011 with the Green Bay Packers; made 10 Pro Bowls

PERSONAL HIGHLIGHTS: invented a touchdown celebration called The Belt; won a National Basketball Association (NBA) title as part owner of the Milwaukee Bucks in 2018; is one of the oldest active players in the NFL

Rodgers runs for a touchdown on January 1, 2023.

 With the Packers ahead 17–3 late in the second quarter, Rodgers went to work. He took his team down the field. He ended the drive when he threw a 21-yard touchdown pass to teammate Robert Tonyan.

 Green Bay was well on its way to a win. But Rodgers was not done. He ran for a two-yard touchdown in the second half. That gave his team a huge 41–3 lead. The Vikings scored two late touchdowns to make the final score 41–17.

"It's been an interesting year," Rodgers said after the win. "It hasn't been my best football at times. But I've been asked to step up my leadership, and be someone the guys can count on to keep it together."

Green Bay fans had seen him come up big in many games before. Rodgers is one of the best quarterbacks to ever play pro football. But before he turned pro, many people didn't know how good he would become.

Rodgers looks on during the January 1, 2023, game against the Vikings

CHAPTER 1

CHILDHOOD

Aaron Rodgers was born on December 2, 1983, to Darla and Edward Rodgers. He grew up in Chico, California, with his older brother, Luke, and his younger brother, Jordan. Their father had played football for California State University, Chico. He wanted his sons to be active in sports.

Aaron loved sports from an early age. When he was two, he would sit and watch NFL games from start to finish. NFL games last about three hours. Aaron also showed early on that he had talent for the sport. When he was five, he could throw a football through a hanging tire.

Aaron (*center right*) celebrates with family after winning the 2011 Super Bowl.

Growing up, Aaron played different sports such as baseball and basketball. His family also moved around. After leaving Chico, they lived in Ukiah, California. Then they moved to Beaverton, Oregon.

When Aaron was a teenager, his family moved back to Chico. He started playing football at Pleasant Valley High School. Though some doubted him due to his small size, he did well at the sport. As a freshman, he was only 5 feet 3 (1.6 m). But he once threw for six touchdowns in a single game!

Aaron (*right*) and his parents react to his selection by the Green Bay Packers in the 2005 NFL Draft.

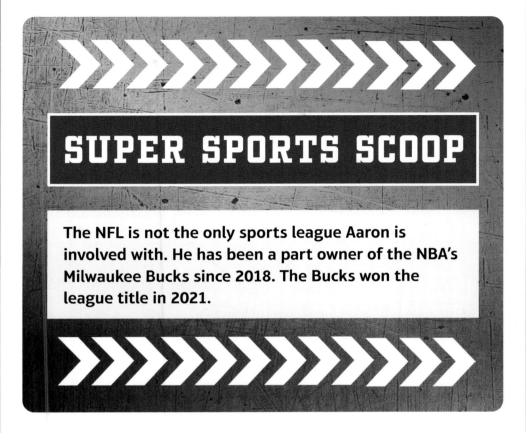

SUPER SPORTS SCOOP

The NFL is not the only sports league Aaron is involved with. He has been a part owner of the NBA's Milwaukee Bucks since 2018. The Bucks won the league title in 2021.

In his final year of high school, Aaron wanted to give up football. He thought he was too small to play. And no Division 1 colleges had offered him a scholarship. Division 1 is the top level of college sports in the US.

Disappointed by the lack of offers, Aaron thought about becoming a pro baseball player instead. He was a good pitcher. But Aaron knew that he could still be a great football player after high school. He just needed a chance to prove it.

In 2002, a coach from Butte College in California wanted Aaron to try out for the team. Butte College was about 15 minutes from Aaron's home in Chico. It didn't matter to Aaron who else was on the Butte College football team. "I don't really care who you got coming back," Aaron told the coach. "[The] only thing that I'll ask is you give me a legitimate chance to start."

The coach agreed. Aaron had the chance to play college football. And he was ready to show what he could do.

Signs at Butte College in California

CHAPTER 2

PROVING HIMSELF AGAIN

It didn't take Rodgers long to prove himself at Butte College. During his first year, he led the team to a 10–1 record and threw for 26 touchdowns. He also helped the team win the conference championship. After that, people paid more attention to Rodgers.

The Golden Bears from the University of California, Berkeley, offered him a scholarship. The school has a Division 1 football team. Rodgers joined the team in 2003.

Rodgers plays for the Golden Bears in 2003.

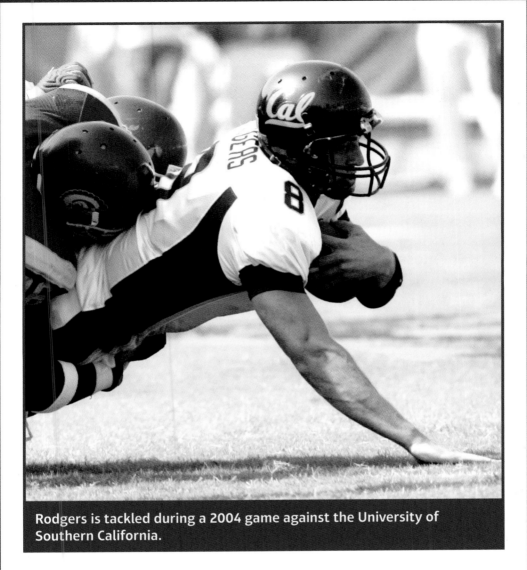

Rodgers is tackled during a 2004 game against the University of Southern California.

With the Golden Bears, Rodgers became a stronger player and leader. In his first season, he became the team's top quarterback. The following season, he helped the team win 10 of its 12 regular season games.

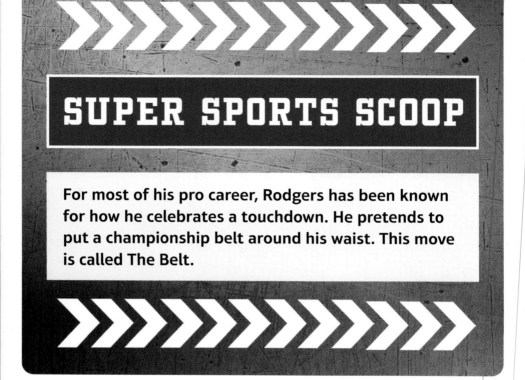

Rodgers played two seasons with the Golden Bears. He could have played one more year of college football. But he decided he was ready to go pro.

Some people thought Rodgers would be the top pick in the 2005 NFL Draft. The team that he had loved growing up, the San Francisco 49ers, had the first pick. Rodgers wanted to play for San Francisco. But they drafted another quarterback instead.

Rodgers was the 24th player drafted. The Green Bay Packers picked him. When asked how he felt about not being chosen by San Francisco, Rodgers said, "[I'm] not as disappointed as the 49ers will be that they didn't draft me," he said.

Rodgers (*left*) with Packers general manager Ted Thompson during the 2005 NFL Draft

CHAPTER 3

NFL SUPERSTAR

Rodgers joined the Green Bay Packers in 2005. Although he had been the best quarterback on his team in college, it would take him a few years to prove that he could be a star as a pro. When he came to Green Bay, the Packers already had another great quarterback, Brett Favre. Rodgers had to sit and wait for his chance to shine.

His chance came in 2007 after Favre retired from the Packers. Rodgers became the team's top quarterback. Favre later changed his mind about retiring and wanted to keep playing. But he was traded to the New York Jets.

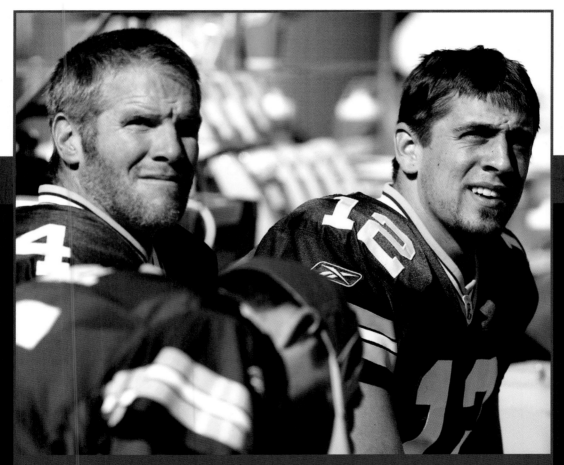

Rodgers (*right*) and Brett Favre (*left*) watch from the sideline during a game in 2005.

"I know I'm capable of reaching greatness," Rodgers said early in his pro career. "And I'm expecting to reach that level."

Rodgers throws the ball during a 2005 practice with the Packers.

SUPER SPORTS SCOOP

Rodgers's brother Jordan hoped to become a quarterback in the NFL. Jordan tried out for three different teams: the Jacksonville Jaguars, Tampa Bay Buccaneers, and Miami Dolphins. But he never played a game in the league.

Rodgers reached his goal in 2011. That year, he led the Packers to the Super Bowl. He threw three touchdown passes to help the Packers beat the Pittsburgh Steelers 31–25. Rodgers was named the Super Bowl MVP.

Rodgers played more than 220 games with the Packers over 18 seasons. During that time, he was named the league MVP four times. And he was picked to play in the Pro Bowl 10 times. The Pro Bowl is a yearly game with the NFL's best players.

Rodgers played his final season with the Packers in 2022. But his pro career was not done yet.

Rodgers holds the Super Bowl MVP trophy after the 2011 Super Bowl.

CHAPTER 4

WHAT'S NEXT

In April 2023, the Packers traded Rodgers to the New York Jets. He signed a two-year deal with the team. But things did not get off to a good start for the then 39-year-old quarterback. In his first regular season game with the Jets, Rodgers hurt his ankle.

He left the game and did not return. He later shared that he had torn his Achilles tendon in his left foot. The Achilles tendon connects a person's lower leg muscles to their heel bone. Rodgers had surgery two days after he got hurt.

Rodgers walks off the field after injuring his ankle in 2023.

SUPER SPORTS SCOOP

If football didn't work out for Rodgers, he might have become a pro baseball player. In high school, he could throw a fastball about 90 miles (145 km) per hour. The average speed of a fastball in pro baseball is about 93 miles (150 km) per hour.

Most NFL players retire before the age of 30. Rodgers wants to return to the field and play for the Jets when he is healed. But he does not know when that might be. "Can I . . . play at the level that I'm capable of playing?" Rodgers asked. "Can I protect myself? Can I move around the way I want to move around?"

Rodgers worked hard to heal from his injury. He wants to show Jets fans that he is still one of the best in the NFL. They can't wait to see what he does next, both on and off the field.

Rodgers watches a Jets game from the sideline in 2023.

Rodgers prepares to throw the ball while warming up for a game in 2023.

AARON RODGERS CAREER STATS

GAMES PLAYED:

231

PASSES ATTEMPTED:

7,661

PASSES COMPLETED:

5,001

PASSING TOUCHDOWNS:

475

RUSHING TOUCHDOWNS:

35

Stats are accurate through the 2023 NFL season.

GLOSSARY

Division 1: the highest level of college sports in the US

draft: when teams take turns choosing new players

MVP: short for *most valuable player*

pass: when a football player, usually a quarterback, throws the ball to a teammate

pro: short for *professional*, taking part in an activity to make money

Pro Bowl: the NFL's all-star game

quarterback: the player on a football team that controls the offense and throws passes

record: the number of wins and losses a team has

rival: a player or team that tries to defeat or be more successful than another

scholarship: money that a school or another group gives to students to help pay for their education

Super Bowl: the championship game played each year between two NFL teams

SOURCE NOTES

7   Safid Deen, "Aaron Rodgers Kept the Faith to Turn Packers' Disappointing Year into Postseason Shot," *USA Today*, January 1, 2023, https://www.usatoday.com/story/sports/nfl /packers/2023/01/01/packers-season-going-how-aaron-rodgers -envisioned-after-4-8-start/10979455002/.

12 The Athletic NFL Staff, "The NFL 100: From Derrick Brooks to Tom Brady, The Athletic Finds the Best Players in Football History," *The Athletic*, September 8, 2021, https://theathletic .com/2685622/2021/09/08/the-nfl-100-from-derrick-brooks -to-tom-brady-the-athletic-finds-the-best-players-in-football -history/.

17 Jake Curtis, "Remembering Aaron Rodgers' Classic Quote from 2005 NFL Draft," SI.com, April 30, 2021, https://www .si.com/college/cal/news/aaron-rodgers-2005-draft.

20 George Johnson and Allan Maki, *NFL Heroes: The 100 Greatest Players of All Time*, (Buffalo: Firefly Books, 2022), 138-139.

25 The Athletic Staff, "Aaron Rodgers Says 2023 Return Depends on His Health: 'I'm Not at an Ability to Play at This Point,'" *The Athletic*, November 28, 2023, https://theathletic.com /5096751/2023/11/28/jets-aaron-rodgers-injury-update/.

LEARN MORE

Anderson, Josh. *Inside the Green Bay Packers*. Minneapolis: Lerner Publications, 2024.

ESPN: Aaron Rodgers
https://www.espn.com/nfl/player/_/id/8439/aaron-rodgers

Lowe, Alexander. *G.O.A.T. Football Quarterbacks*. Minneapolis: Lerner Publications, 2023.

NFL: Aaron Rodgers
https://www.nfl.com/players/aaron-rodgers/

Scheffer, Janie. *The New York Jets*. Minneapolis: Bellwether Media, 2024.

Sports Illustrated Kids: Football
https://www.sikids.com/football

INDEX

PHOTO ACKNOWLEDGMENTS

Images: AP Photo/Mike Roemer, pp. 4, 17, 20; AP Photo/Morry Gash, p. 6; AP Photo/Scott Boehm, p. 7; GH Maps/Alamy, p. 8; AP Photo/Kevin Terrell, p. 9; AP Photo/Julie Jacobson, p. 10; Anda Chu/Digital First Media/East Bay Times/Getty Images, p. 12; AP Photo/Jeff Chiu, p. 13; AP Photo/Kevin Reece, p. 14; AP Photo/Chris Carlson, p. 15; AP Photo/David Stluka, p. 18; AP Photo/Joe Robbins, p. 19; Streeter Lecka/Getty Images, p. 22; Ryan Kang/Getty Images, pp. 23, 27; Michael Owens/Getty Images, p. 24; Dustin Satloff/Getty Images, p. 26.

Cover: AP Photo/Scott Boehm.